Impressum
Verlag: BABADADA GmbH, Nedderfeld 112 , 22529 Hamburg
Geschäftsführer / Verlagsleitung: Harald Hof
Druck: Books on Demand GmbH, In de Tarpen 42, 22848 Norderstedt

Imprint
Publisher: BABADADA GmbH, Nedderfeld 112 , 22529 Hamburg, Germany
Managing Director / Publishing direction: Harald Hof
Print: Books on Demand GmbH, In de Tarpen 42, 22848 Norderstedt

siklyovimasko than
classroom

ulavibe vordon
divide

186/2

tabla
board

školaki avlin
school yard

sikavno
teacher

lil
paper

hramovibe
write

kalemi tintasa
pen

masa butyake
desk

lenyiri
ruler

lil
book

siklo
pupil

dumeski tašna

satchel

kalemengi kutia

pencil case

kalemi

pencil

kalemengi čhurori

pencil sharpener

kosimaski guma

rubber

čitrimasko bloko

drawing pad

čitribe

drawing

boyimaski frča

paintbrush

boyimaski kutia

paint box

kata

scissors

lepako

glue

bukjardarimasko lil

exercise book

khereski buti

homework

gendo

number

džide

add

ikal

subtract

multiplicirin

multiply

kalkulirin

calculate

hramome lil

letter

alfabeta

alphabet

lafo

word

škola - school

3

teksti

text

drabaribe

read

kreda

chalk

lekciya

lesson

Klasesko registro

register

egzameni

examination

sertifikato

certificate

školaki uniforma

school uniform

edukacia

education

enciklopedia

encyclopedia

univerziteto

university

mikroskopo

microscope

mapa

map

korpa čhudimaske lila

waste-paper basket

hoteli
hotel

Lačhi blevel!
hostel

biro baši devize
currency exchange office

koferi
suitcase

vordon
car

ćhib

language

va / na

yes / no

Okay

Okay

Namaste

hello

tumači

translator

Ov sasto

Thank you

Kozom si...?

how much is...?

Na havava

I don´t get it

problemo

problem

Lačhi rat!

Good evening!

Lačhi javin!

Good morning!

Lačhi rat!

Good night!

ačhon Devlesa

goodbye

dromeski sikavin

direction

bagaži

luggage

gono

bag

dumesko gono

backpack

misafiri

guest

kamara

room

sovimasko gono

sleeping bag

cerha

tent

turistikani informacia

tourist information

plaža

beach

kreditno kartica

credit card

javinako habe

breakfast

kušluko

lunch

ratyako habe

dinner

karta

Ticket

elevatori

elevator

marka

stamp

simantra

border

adetia

customs

ambasada

embassy

viza

visa

pašaporti

passport

avioni
airplane

baro vapori
ship

jagako motori
fire truck

autobusi
bus

kamionia
truck

vapori ko motori
motorboat

biciklo
bike

vordon
car

feri vapori
ferry

vapori
boat

motorciklo
motorbike

policiako vordon
police car

prastamasko vordon
racing car

rentakar
rental car

8

ulavibe vordon

car sharing

rumosardo kamioni

tow truck

kamionengo than

garbage truck

motori

engine

petroli

fuel

petrolesko stasioni

fuel station

trafikoskere išaretia

traffic sign

trafiko

traffic

baro trafiko

traffic jam

vordonesko parkirimasko than

parking lot

pampurengo stasioni

train station

kamionia

tracks

pampuri

train

tramvaj

tram

vagoni

wagon

helikopteri

helicopter

aeroporti

airport

kula

tower

dromarutno

passenger

kontejneri

container

kartoni

carton

vordonoro

cart

sevli

basket

urjalipasko starto /
urjalipasko agor

take off / land

diz

city

gav

village

dizyako centro

city center

kher

house

koliba
hut

apartmani
apartment

pampurengo stasioni
train station

dizyaki sala
city hall

muzeji
museum

škola
school

univerziteto

university

banka

bank

hospitalo

hospital

hoteli

hotel

apoteka

pharmacy

ofiso

office

lil bikinimasko than

book shop

dukyano

shop

lulugengo bikinutno

flower shop

supermarket

supermarket

kurko

market

baro bikinimasko kher

department store

mačhengo astarutno

fishmonger's shop

kinimasko centro

mall

vaporengo ačhovimasko
than

harbor

parko

park

klupa

bench

purt

bridge

merdevenya

stairs

metro stasioni

subway

tuneli

tunnel

autobuseski adžikerin

bus stop

bar

bar

restorani

restaurant

poštako mohto

postbox

dromesko išareti

street sign

parking than

parking meter

zoo

zoo

nangyovimasko bazeni

swimming pool

džamiya

mosque

farma

farm

melalipe

pollution

limorengo than

cemetery

khangeri

church

khelimasko than

playground

hramo

temple

pejžaži

landscape

patrin
leaf

išareti
signpost

drom
path

livazin
meadow

bar
stone

phiravno
hiker

kašt
tree

len
river

čar
grass

luludi
flower

harno than
valley

bairi
hill

devrijal
lake

veš
forest

mulano than
desert

vulkano
volcano

saraji
castle

renkali badalin
rainbow

gaba
mushroom

palma kašt
palm tree

sivrija
mosquito

mak
fly

karandža
ant

birumni
bee

pauko
spider

buba

beetle

žamba

frog

ververica

squirrel

kanzauri

hedgehog

šošoj

hare

buf

owl

pakšin

bird

lebedi

swan

bali

boar

eleno

deer

eleno

moose

pani garavin

dam

bavlalaki turbina

wind turbine

solarno paneli

solar panel

klima

climate

kelneri
waiter

menije
menu

sandaliya
chair

čorba
soup

pica
pizza

poftaneski salfetka
tablecloth

habasko alati
cutlery

avgo habe

starter

šerutno habe

main course

gudlimata

dessert

piiba

drinks

habe

food

šiša

bottle

fast food

fast food

sokakongo habe

street food

čajniko

teapot

šekereskoro čaroro

sugar bowl

porcia

portion

makina vaš espresso

espresso machine

uči sandaliya

high chair

esapi

bill

apladiya

tray

čhuri

knife

vilyuška

fork

roj

spoon

čajeski roj

teaspoon

salfetka

serviette

tahtai

glass

čaro
plate

čaro čorbake
soup plate

hor čaro
saucer

sosi
sauce

londesko čaroro
salt shaker

kale biberesko pišlo
pepper mill

šut
vinegar

zejtini
oil

začinia
spices

kečap
ketchup

senf
mustard

majonezi
mayonnaise

specialno oferta
special offer

mušteriya
customer

thudeske butya
dairy products

emiši
fruit

vordonoro
shopping cart

kasapi

butcher's shop

furuna

bakery

ladavipe

weigh

zarzavati

vegetables

masesko rolati

meat

pahome habe

frozen food

šudro mas

cold cuts

konzerva

canned food

thovimasko prašako

detergent

gudlimata

candy

khereske butya

household products

užarimaske butya

cleaning products

bikinutno

sales representative

kasapi

cash register

kasieri

cashier

kinimaski patrin

shopping list

putarimaske satura

opening hours

lovengi tašna

wallet

kreditno kartica

credit card

gono

bag

plastikano gono

plastic bag

pani

water

džus

juice

thud

milk

kola

coke

mol

wine

bira

beer

alkohol

alcohol

kakao

cocoa

čaj

tea

kafa

coffee

espresso

espresso

cappuccino

cappuccino

banana

banana

phabaj

apple

portokali

orange

kavuni

melon

limoni

lemon

karota

carrot

sir

garlic

bambusi

bamboo

purum

onion

gaba

mushroom

akhora

nuts

humereske butya

noodles

špageti

spaghetti

rezo

rice

salata

salad

čipsi

fries

peke kompiria

fried potatoes

pica

pizza

hamburger

hamburger

sendviči

sandwich

kotleti

escalope

žamboni

ham

salama

salami

goja

sausage

khajnako mas

chicken

peko

roast

mačho

fish

popara

porridge oats

musli

muesli

kornfleks

cornflakes

varo

flour

kroasani

croissant

masesko rolati

bread roll

maro

bread

tosti

toast

biskotia

cookies

puteri

butter

urda

curd

torta

cake

jaro

egg

peke jare

fried egg

kiral

cheese

šudro gudlo

ice cream

šekeri

sugar

avgin

honey

džem

jelly

čokoladaki krema

nougat cream

kari

curry

farmako kher
farm house

hasari
barn

bale pus
straw bale

umal
field

grast
horse

indžarimasko vordon
trailer

grastoro
foal

traktori
tractor

her
donkey

bakhroro
lamb

bakhroro
sheep

buzno
goat

guruvni
cow

guruvoro
calf

balo
pig

baloro
piglet

guruv
bull

papin

goose

payka

duck

pilička

chick

khayni

hen

bašno

cockerel

baro germuso

rat

bilika

cat

germuso

mouse

guruv

ox

džukel

dog

džukelesko kher

dog house

žardina

garden hose

panyarimaski kanta

watering can

aindžako kidimasko alati

scythe

plugo

plow

srpo

sickle

motika

hoe

aindžaki vilyuška

pitchfork

tover

axe

vordonoro phiravutno

pushcart

balani

trough

thudeski šiša

milk can

harari

sack

trujalutni

fence

jahri

stable

haryalo kher

greenhouse

phuv

soil

seme

seed

gyubre

fertilizer

aindžako kidipe

combine harvester

farma - farm

kidibe aindž

harvest

harmani

harvest

phuvaki phabaj

yams

giv

wheat

soja

soya

kompiri

potato

mumuruzi

corn

šarlagani

rapeseed

emišengo kašt

fruit tree

Kasava

manioc

giveskere javinlukoja

grain

odžako
chimney

učharin khereski
roof

cevka
downspout

pendžarka
window

garaža
garage

udaresko zili
doorbell

udar
door

gunoeski korpa
trash can

mohto
mailbox

bavča
garden

bešimaski kamara

living room

banya

bathroom

kujna

kitchen

sovimasko than

bedroom

čhavengi kamara

kids room

than hajbaske rakjako habe

dining room

kati

floor

duvari

wall

tavano

ceiling

špajzi

cellar

sauna

sauna

terasa

balcony

terasa

terrace

bazeni

pool

čar harnyarimaski makina

lawn mower

patrin

sheet

čaršafia

bedspread

kreveto

bed

šulavni

broom

korpa

bucket

elektrikani phabarin

switch

kher - house

tapeta
wallpaper

tasviri
picture

lamba
lamp

rafti
shelf

ormari
cabinet

jagako than
fireplace

televiziya
television

luludi
flower

šerand
cushion

vazna
vase

sofa
sofa

durutni komanda
remote control

kilimi
carpet

perde
drape

masa
table

sandaliya
chair

kunajka sandaliya
rocking chair

fotelya
armchair

lil

book

kebe

blanket

dekoraciya

decoration

kašta phabarimaske

firewood

filmi

film

stereo ašunimaske butya

stereo system

nahtari

key

gazeta

newspaper

frčaja bojakeribe

painting

posteri

poster

radio

radio

hramovimasko bloko

notebook

elektrikani šulavni

vacuum cleaner

kaktusi

cactus

momoli

candle

frižideri
fridge

mikrodalgaki rerna
microwave oven

kujnako kantari
kitchen scales

tosteri
toaster

detergenti
laundry detergent

furna
stove

hor pahonimaski komora
freezer

gunoeski korpa
trash can

detergenti čarenge
dishwasher

keravimasko than
cooker

čaro
pot

sastrnali tendžera
cast-iron pot

vok cihani
wok / kadai

tava
pan

elektrikano bokali
kettle

tendžera ki para

steamer

tepsija

baking tray

čare

crockery

bareder fildžano

mug

čaro

bowl

kinakere habaskere kaštore

chopsticks

fioka

ladle

špatula

spatula

vastesko mikseri

whisk

cedimasko čaro

strainer

porizen

sieve

rende

grater

avano

mortar

skara

barbecue

puteribe jag

fireplace

čhinimaski tabla

chopping board

oklagia

rolling pin

puterimasko alati

corkscrew

konzerva

can

konzervako puterutno

can opener

čaresko ikerutno

oven cloth

lavabo

sink

frča

brush

sungeri

sponge

mikseri

blender

hor pahonimasko frižideri

deep freezer

bebeski šiša

baby bottle

češma

tap

tuširibe
shower

tataripe
heating

peškiri
towel

tuširimaski perda
shower curtain

nanyovibe sapuneske balonencar
bubble bath

kada nanyovimaske
bathtub

tahtai
glass

makina thovimaske šeja
washing machine

češma
tap

pločke
tiles

turako
potty

lavabo
sink

toaleti
toilet

toaleti bešimasa ko pundre
squat toilet

bide
bidet

pisoari
urinal

toaletesko lil
toilet paper

frča toaleteske
toilet brush

danda thovimaski frča
....
toothbrush

danda thovimaski krema
....
toothpaste

dandesko thav
....
dental floss

thovibe danda
....
wash

vasteskoro tuši
....
hand shower

tuši
....
douche

lavabo
....
basin

dumeski frča
....
back brush

sapuni
....
soap

tuširimasko geli
....
shower gel

šamponi
....
shampoo

flanela
....
flannel

kada ćidimaske pani
....
drain

krema
....
creme

dezodoransi
....
deodorant

ajna

mirror

vasteski ajna

hand mirror

žileti moravimaske

razor

moravimaski pena

shaving foam

palal muravimaski krema

aftershave

kanglik

comb

frča

brush

feni balenge

hair-dryer

sprej balenge

hairspray

šminka

makeup

karmini

lipstick

oja najenge

nail varnish

pamuko pošom

cotton wool

kata najenge

nail scissors

parfemi

perfume

gono thovimaske

washbag

sandaliya

stool

tereziya

weighing scales

bademantili

bathrobe

gumena kalcunya

rubber gloves

tamponi

tampon

toaletno lil

sanitary towel

hemikano toaleti

chemical toilet

alarmesko sato
alarm clock

mangli khelutni
cuddly toy

vordonora khelimaske
toy car

tropalka
rattle

bebedžikongo kher
doll's house

bakšiši
present

baloni

balloon

kreveto

bed

bebengo vordon

stroller

špili karte

deck of cards

ker-rumin khelin

jigsaw

komikano lil

comic

lego kocke

lego bricks

kocke khelimaske

toy blocks

akciaki figura

action figure

bodi bebeske

romper suit

frizbi

frisbee

mobile

mobile

masa khelimaske

board game

zari

dice

pampuri khelimaske

model train set

cucla

pacifier

bahlana

party

tasvirengo lil

picture book

topka

ball

bebedžiko

doll

khelibe

play

pošikako than
....
sandpit

kuna
....
swing

khelimaske butya
....
toys

konzola video khelimaske
....
video game console

triciklo
....
tricycle

poftaneski ričini
....
teddy bear

garderoba
....
wardrobe

šeja

clothing

kalcunya
....
socks

khuvde kalcunya
....
stockings

hulahopke
....
tights

momija
scarf

kaiši
belt

čadori
umbrella

maica
t-shirt

čizme
boots

papuče
slippers

trenerke
sneakers

sandale

sandals

menije

shoes

gumena čizme

rubber boots

sostenya

underwear

eleko

bra

jeleko

undershirt

bodi

body

pantalonya

pants

farmerke

jeans

suknya

skirt

bluza

blouse

gat

shirt

puloveri

pullover

dukseri

sweater

harno kaputi

blazer

džeketi

jacket

kaputi

coat

biršimdesko mantili

raincoat

kostimi

costume

fustano

dress

prandinako fustano

wedding dress

kostumi

suit

rakjako fustano

nightgown

pižame

pajamas

sari

sari

momija šereske

headscarf

turbani

turban

burka

burka

kaftani

kaftan

abaya

abaya

nangyovimaske šeja

swimsuit

buxle pantolonya

trunks

harne pantolonya

shorts

sporteske trenerke

tracksuit

kecelya

apron

vasteske kalcunya

gloves

kopča

button

gjuzlukya

glasses

belegziya

bracelet

mirikle

necklace

angrustik

ring

čeni

earring

stadik

cap

kaputeski čiviya

coat hanger

stadik

hat

kravata

tie

patenti

zip

kaciga

helmet

dandenge proteze

braces

školaki uniforma

school uniform

uniforma

uniform

ligarka
....
bib

cucla
....
pacifier

pherno
....
diaper

serveri
server

raftija dokumentenca
filing cabinet

printeri
printer

lil
paper

monitori
monitor

masa butyake
desk

mausi
mouse

folderi
folder

tastatura
keyboard

korpa čhudimaske lila
waste-paper basket

kompjuteri
computer

sandaliya
chair

fildžano kafake
....
coffee mug

kalkulatori
....
calculator

internet
....
internet

laptop

laptop

lil

letter

mesaži

message

mobilno telefono

cell phone

netvorko

network

kopirimaski makina

photocopier

softveri

software

telefono

telephone

štekeri

plug socket

faks makina

fax machine

formulari

form

dokumento

document

kinibe

buy

pokinibe

pay

kino-bikinibe

trade

love

money

dolari

dollar

euro

euro

jeni

yen

rublya

rouble

švajcariako franko

Swiss franc

renminbi juan

renminbi yuan

rupija

rupee

lovengo automati

cash point

biro baši devize

currency exchange office

somnakaj

gold

rup

silver

petroli

oil

energia

energy

fiyati

price

kontrakto

contract

taksa

tax

berzaki akcija

stock

butikeribe

work

butyarno

employee

butyako dendutno

employer

fabrika

factory

dukyano

shop

Policiako oficero
police officer

jagako aćhavutno
fireman

habekerutno
cook

doktoro
doctor

piloti
pilot

bavčako butyarno
gardener

tišleri
carpenter

šnajderka
seamstress

krisuno
judge

hemičari
chemist

akteri
actor

autobusesko šoferi

bus driver

taksisti

taxi driver

mačhengo astarutno

fisherman

užarutni

cleaning lady

učharinengo kerutno

roofer

kelneri

waiter

avdžija

hunter

tasvirkerutno

painter

furnadžia

baker

elektrikako phirno

electrician

tamirutno

builder

inžinjeri

engineer

kasapi

butcher

panjesko butyarno

plumber

poštari

postman

askeri

soldier

arhitekto

architect

kasieri

cashier

luludyari

florist

frizeri

hairdresser

kondukteri

conductor

mekanisti

mechanic

kapetani

captain

dandengo saslyarno

dentist

vigjanalo manuš

scientist

rabini

rabbi

imami

imam

rašaj

monk

rašaj

pastor

čekiči
hammer

silavja
pliers

šrafcigeri
screwdriver

mekanikane nahtaria
wrench

fakeli
torch

hrandimasko alati
excavator

alateski kutia
toolbox

merdeveni
ladder

pila
saw

karfa
nails

posavin
drill

lačharkeribe
repair

lopata
shovel

Naleti!
Damn!

vatrali
dustpan

lonco bojimaske
paint can

šrafja
screws

muzikane instrumentia
musical instruments

bare avazesko šunutno
loud speaker

davulenge butya
drum set

gitara
guitar

duplo bas
double bass

truba
trumpet

piano
piano

kemana
violin

bas
bass

timpani
timpani

davulia
drums

sintisajzeri
keyboard

saksafoni
saxophone

flejta
flute

mikrofoni
microphone

tigari
tiger

khuvin
entrance

kafezi
cage

zebra nakhimaski
zebra

hajvanengo parvaripe
animal feed

panda
panda

hajvania
animals

elefanti
elephant

kenguri
kangaroo

rino
rhino

gorila
gorilla

ričini
bear

kamila

camel

ostriga

ostrich

aslani

lion

majmuni

monkey

flamingo

flamingo

papagali

parrot

polarno ričini

polar bear

pingvini

penguin

ajkula

shark

pauno

peacock

sap

snake

krokodilo

crocodile

zoo arakhutno

zookeeper

foka

seal

jaguari

jaguar

poni

pony

leopardi

leopard

hipo

hippo

žirafa

giraffe

zorale kandžengi paškin

eagle

bali

boar

mačho

fish

želka

turtle

morži

walrus

lumri

fox

gazela

gazelle

Amerikako fudbali
American football

biciklizmo
cycling

tenis
tennis

basketboli
basketball

nangjovibe
swimming

boksi
boxing

hokej ko paho
ice hockey

fudbali
....
soccer

badmington
....
badminton

atletika
....
athletics

vasteskoboli
....
handball

skiibe
....
skiing

polo
....
polo

asaibe
laugh

hutibe
jump

deibe angali
hug

giljavibe
sing

phiribe
walk

dikhibe suno
dream

azirikeribe
pray

čumíbe
kiss

hramovibe

write

čitribe

draw

sikavibe

show

cidljaribe

push

deibe

give

leibe

take

isibe

have

keribe

do

te ovel

be

tergyovibe

stand

prastaibe

run

cidibe

pull

čhudibe

throw

peribe

fall

hovavibe

lie

adžikeribe

wait

phiravibe

carry

bešibe

sit

urjavibe

get dressed

sovibe

sleep

džangavibe

wake up

dikhibe ko

look at

rovibe

cry

čalavibe

stroke

uhlavibr

comb

vakeribe

talk

haljovibe

understand

puč

ask

šunibe

listen

piibe

drink

habe

eat

užaribe

tidy up

kamibe

love

keribe habe

cook

paldibe vordon

drive

urjalibe

fly

vaporea džaibe

sail

kalkulirin

calculate

drabaribe

read

sikljovibe

learn

butikeribe

work

prandibe

marry

suvibe

sew

thovibe danda

brush teeth

mudaribe

kill

piibe dahani

smoke

bičhalibe

send

mami
grandmother

papu
grandfather

dat
father

daj
mother

bebe
baby

čhaj
daughter

čhavo
son

misafiri

guest

bibi

aunt

kako

uncle

phral

brother

phen

sister

čekat
forehead

jakh
eye

piko
shoulder

naj
finger

muj
face

vilica
chin

vast
hand

čuči
breast

pundro
leg

musik
arm

bebe
....
baby

murš
....
man

džuvli
....
woman

čhaj
....
girl

ćhavo
....
boy

šero
....
head

dumo

back

maškar

belly

pupko

navel

pundrenge naja

toe

patum

heel

kokalo

bone

kuko

hip

koč

knee

lahci

elbow

nakh

nose

bul

buttocks

mortik

skin

čham

cheek

kan

ear

voš

lip

muj

mouth

danda

tooth

ćhib

tongue

godi

brain

vilo

heart

muskulo

muscle

kolin

lung

buko

liver

vogi

stomach

bubrekora

kidneys

seks

sex

kondomi

condom

yarengi kletka

ovum

sperma

semen

khamnipe

pregnancy

trupo - body

menstruaciya

menstruation

vagina

vagina

penis

penis

phov

eyebrow

bala

hair

men

neck

hospitalo
hospital

medicinako vordon
ambulance

invalidsko vordon
wheelchair

phagipe
fracture

doktoro

doctor

sigyarimaski kamara

emergency room

medicinaki phen

nurse

sigyaripen

emergency

ki koma

unconscious

dukh

pain

dukhavipen

injury

ratvaripe

bleeding

infrakto

heart attack

šlog

stroke

alergiya

allergy

khuinibe

cough

tinanipe

fever

gripa

flu

diyarea

diarrhea

šereski dukh

headache

kanceri

cancer

diyabetes

diabetes

operaciya

surgeon

skalperi

scalpel

operaciya

operation

CT

CT

rentgen

x-ray

ultra avazo

ultrasound

mujeski maska

face mask

nasvalipe

disease

adžukyarimasko than

waiting room

paterica

crutch

flastero

plaster

phandimaski gaza

bandage

inyekciya

injection

stetoskopo

stethoscope

tregero

stretcher

klinicko termometro

clinical thermometer

biyanipe

birth

baro thulipe

overweight

hospitalo - hospital

ašunimasko aparato

hearing aid

dezinfekciako

disinfectant

infekciya

infection

viruso

virus

HIV / SIDA

HIV / AIDS

medicina

medicine

vakcinaciya

vaccination

tabletura

tablets

hapi

pill

sigyarimasko akharipe

emergency call

monitori vaš učo pretisak

blood pressure monitor

nasvalo / sasto

ill / healthy

Mažutisar!

Help!

alarmo

alarm

atako

assault

atako

attack

dar buti

danger

sigyarimasko iklyovipen

emergency exit

Bari jag!

Fire!

mamuj jagako aparati

fire extinguisher

bibax

accident

butya avgo ažutimaske

first-aid kit

SOS

SOS

Policia

police

Evropa

Europe

Utarali Amerika

North America

Purabali Amerika

South America

Afrika

Africa

Azija

Asia

Australia

Australia

Atlantiko

Atlantic

Pacifiko

Pacific

Indiako Okeano

Indian Ocean

Antarktikosko Okeano

Antarctic Ocean

Arktikosko Okeano

Arctic Ocean

Utaralo poli

North pole

Purabalo poli

South pole

Antarktiko

Antarctica

phuv

earth

phuv

land

samudra

sea

džaziri

island

nacija

nation

raštra

state

saatosko gendo

clock face

saatoski sikavni

hour hand

dakikongi sikavni

minute hand

ekundarno saatoski sikavin

second hand

Kozom si o saato?

What time is it?

dive

day

vrama

time

akana

now

digitalno saato

digital watch

dakika

minute

časo

hour

Lujin
Monday

trintodi
Wednesday

Paraskin
Friday

Dujtodi
Tuesday

Savato
Saturday

Štartodi
Thursday

Purano kurko
Sunday

erati

yesterday

avdive

today

tajsa

tomorrow

javin

morning

ekvaš dive

noon

blevel

evening

butyarne divesa

workdays

vikend

weekend

biršim
rain

renkali badalin
rainbow

iv
snow

bavlal
wind

anglonilaj
spring

palonilaj
fall

nilaj
summer

ivend
winter

4.APRIL	11°	☀
5.APRIL	4°	⛅
6.APRIL	13°	⛅
7.APRIL	8°	☀
8.APRIL	10°	☀

vramakoro vakeribe

weather forecast

termometro

thermometer

khamalo

sunshine

badal

cloud

muhi

fog

nemlime hava

humidity

šemšekoja

lightning

šemšekosko čalavibe

thunder

bura

storm

kijameti

hail

monsuni

monsoon

baro pani

flood

paho

ice

Januaro

January

Februaro

February

Marto

March

Aprilo

April

Majo

May

Juno

June

Julo

July

Augusto

August

berš - year

Septembro

September

Oktombro

October

Novembro

November

Dekembro

December

forme

shapes

rota

circle

kvadrati

square

rektanglo

rectangle

trianglo

triangle

sfera

sphere

kocka

cube

boje
colors

parni
....
white

galbeno
....
yellow

pomarandža
....
orange

roze
....
pink

loli
....
red

lila
....
purple

vunato
....
blue

harjali
....
green

kafeno
....
brown

kuršumlija
....
gray

kali
....
black

opposites

but / hari

a lot / a little

holjame / mudro

angry / calm

šuži / bišuži

beautiful / ugly

starto / agor

beginning / end

baro / tikno

big / small

puterde bojako / phanle bojako

bright / dark

phral / phen

brother / sister

užo / melalo

clean / dirty

sahno / bisahno

complete / incomplete

dive / rat

day / night

mulo / dživdo

dead / alive

buvlo / tank

wide / narrow

hala pe / na hala pe

edible / inedible

džungalo / šukar

evil / kind

bare vogjea / bi vogjea

excited / bored

thulo / kišlo

fat / thin

avgo / paluno

first / last

amal / dušmani

friend / enemy

pherdo / čučo

full / empty

zoralo / kovlo

hard / soft

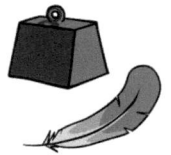

pharo / lokho

heavy / light

bokh / truš

hunger / thirst

nasvalo / sasto

ill / healthy

ilegalno / legalno

illegal / legal

godyaver / bigodyako

intelligent / stupid

bajan / dahin

left / right

paše / dur

near / far

nevo / purano

new / used

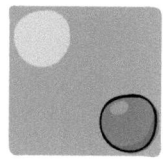

khanči / vareso

nothing / something

phuro / terno

old / young

phabardo / ačhavdo

on / off

puterdo / phanlo

open / closed

mudro / bare avazeskoro

quiet / loud

barvalo / čorolo

rich / poor

čačutno / došalo

right / wrong

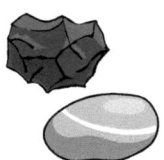

zoralo / kovlo

rough / smooth

mazuni / lošalo

sad / happy

skurto / lungo

short / long

pohari / sigate

slow / fast

sapano / šuko

wet / dry

tato / šudro

warm / cool

mareba / sansari

war / peace

0

zero

zero

1

jek

one

2

duj

two

3

trin

three

4

štar

four

5

panč

five

6

šov

six

7

efta

seven

8

ohto

eight

9

enja

nine

10

deš

ten

11

dešujek

eleven

12	**13**	**14**
dešuduj	dešutrin	dešuštar
twelve	thirteen	fourteen

15	**16**	**17**
dešupanč	dešušov	dešefta
fifteen	sixteen	seventeen

18	**19**	**20**
dešohto	dešenja	biš
eighteen	nineteen	twenty

100	**1.000**	**1.000.000**
šel	milja	milioni
hundred	thousand	million

Anglicko

English

Americko Anglicko

American English

Kinesko Mandarinsko

Chinese Mandarin

Indisko

Hindi

Špansko

Spanish

Francusko

French

Arapsko

Arabic

Rusko

Russian

Portugalsko

Portuguese

Bengalsko

Bengali

Nemicko

German

Japansko

Japanese

thaj

I

tu

you

ov / oj

he / she / it

amen

we

tumen

you

ola

they

ko?

who?

so?

what?

sar?

how?

kote?

where?

kana?

when?

anav

name

palal

behind

andre

in

anglal o

in front of

upral

over

an

on

telal

under

trujal

beside

maškaral

between

than

place